OAK ISLAND

and the Search for Buried Treasure

Joann Hamilton-Barry

NIMBUS
PUBLISHING

Nimbus Publishing Limited
3731 Mackintosh St, Halifax, NS B3K 5A5
(902) 455-4286 nimbus.ca

Printed and bound in Canada

NB1180

Cover photos: Lenn Wagg (Oak Island); Private Collection, Peter Newark Pictures/Bridgeman Images (*Captain Kidd burying treasure* by Howard Pyle).

Design: Jenn Embree

Library and Archives Canada Cataloguing in Publication

Hamilton-Barry, Joann, author
Oak Island : and the search for buried treasure / Joann Hamilton-Barry.
    Includes bibliographical references and index.
    Issued in print and electronic formats.
    ISBN 978-1-77108-342-3 (paperback).—ISBN 978-1-77108-343-0 (pdf)

1. Oak Island (Lunenburg, N.S.)—Juvenile literature. 2. Treasure troves—Nova Scotia—Oak Island (Lunenburg)—History—Juvenile literature. I. Title.

FC2345.O23H36 2015   j622'.190971623   C2015-904329-8
                                                             C2015-904330-1

Canada Council   Conseil des arts
for the Arts   du Canada

Nimbus Publishing acknowledges the financial support for its publishing activities from the Government of Canada through the Canada Book Fund (CBF) and the Canada Council for the Arts, and from the Province of Nova Scotia. We are pleased to work in partnership with the Province of Nova Scotia to develop and promote our creative industries for the benefit of all Nova Scotians.

To my mother, Norma Hamilton, for instilling my love of books and reading.

Table of Contents

Introduction

Lure of Buried Treasure

Very strange, thought Daniel McGinnis as he took a break from his morning of exploring on Oak Island. *Why would someone bother to make such a small clearing here?* He glanced around and noticed that the ground under the only tree looked as if someone had dug a hole and then filled it up again. Very strange indeed. Something else caught his eye. Close to the end of a thick branch of the oak tree was an old **block and tackle**[1]. It was hanging directly over the spot where someone had been digging.

He thought about the clearing, the digging, and the tackle block. Suddenly, all of the clues came together. Daniel McGinnis was sure that he found the spot where Captain Kidd had hidden his treasure. *There has to be pirate gold buried here! What else could it be?* Running off to get his friends John Smith and Anthony Vaughan, he thought, *All we need to do is to dig for a couple of hours. By the end of the day we are going to be very, very rich!*

Many years later, William S. Crooker, who has written many books on Oak Island, said that on that day, the

---

1   Check the glossary on page 74 for all the words you see in yellow.

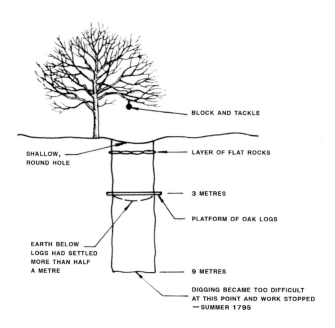

BLOCK AND TACKLE

SHALLOW, ROUND HOLE

LAYER OF FLAT ROCKS

3 METRES

PLATFORM OF OAK LOGS

EARTH BELOW LOGS HAD SETTLED MORE THAN HALF A METRE

9 METRES

DIGGING BECAME TOO DIFFICULT AT THIS POINT AND WORK STOPPED — SUMMER 1795

In the summer of 1795, Daniel McGinnis and his friends were able to dig to a depth of nine metres. To understand how deep they got, a basketball net is about three metres from the ground.

three friends "launched a saga that would claim lives and squander fortunes." Ever since that summer day in 1795, people have been dreaming of finding treasure on Oak Island. Some searchers used nothing but a pick and shovel while others tried machines that could "sniff" out gold. Engineers of every generation have come to the island, sure that they could find the treasure using the most modern methods and the latest technology. So far nothing has worked, but people are still trying to find what is buried in the bottom of that deep hole that has become known as the Money Pit.

Where is Oak Island?

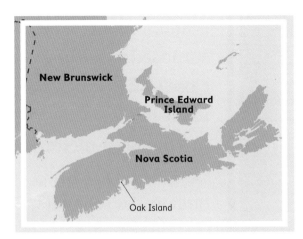

A map of the Maritime provinces, showing Oak Island in Mahone Bay, Nova Scotia.

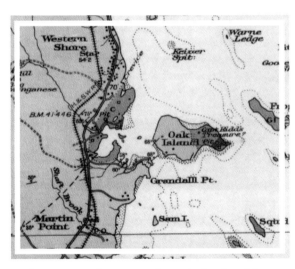

Mahone Bay, showing where Oak Island is joined to Nova Scotia's mainland at Crandall Point.

Chances are you heard of Oak Island before you picked up this book. You may have watched something on TV, checked out a site on the Internet, hunted for pirate gold in a video game, or heard a story of this little island with the big treasure. Oak Island is one of about one hundred islands in Mahone Bay, off the south shore of Nova Scotia. Halifax is about an hour drive away and Chester and Mahone Bay are the

Introduction: Lure of Buried Treasure

Mahone Bay

How many islands are in Mahone Bay? It depends who you ask and what you count as an island. Some of the first books written about Mahone Bay said that it was home to 365 islands, one for every day of the year. This stuck, and most sources say that there are about 350. But to be counted as actual island, a land mass must be above water at high tide. According to the Mahone Islands Conservation Association (MICA), there are 102 islands in Mahone Bay. Oak Island has also been called Island No. 28, Gloucester Island, and Smith's Island.

communities located on either side of the island. You might be surprised to see how close Oak Island is to the mainland. A two hundred-metre causeway, or road, built in 1965 connects the island to the mainland at Western Shore.

From the air, Oak Island looks like a peanut or a question mark. It is just over one kilometre long and about three hundred metres wide where it narrows in at the centre. There are a couple of low hills on the island, lots of rocks, and two swamps. Under the surface are clay, solid rock, and limestone. The island has always been covered with a variety of trees, mostly spruce and other evergreens. Although there are stories about the oak trees disappearing, you will still find lots of them on the island today.

What is Buried on Oak Island?

Could pirate treasure be buried on Oak Island? Does the island hold gold and jewels looted from cities in Central and South America five hundred years ago? Or the crown jewels of France? Could it be the Holy Grail or the treasure of the Knights Templar? Some say that the Money Pit holds priceless historical documents that will amaze the world, or that it may be where the British army hid chests full of gold. There are even people who think that the Money Pit was made by extraterrestrials or that it contains treasure from the lost city of Atlantis.

A postcard showing Oak Island in the late 1800s. Anthony Vaughan, one of the original treasure hunters, lived in the white house seen on the mainland. Today, the Oak Island resort hotel is located in that area.

The Oak Island treasure is rumoured to be worth at least sixty million dollars. People have already spent millions and many have died trying to find what is hidden on the island. Some people think that there is nothing hidden on Oak Island and that the holes discovered there are just sinkholes.

The truth is, no one knows what might be hidden on Oak Island. And until the treasure is found, the search will continue.

Legends and Stories

There are lots of legends and ghost stories about Oak Island. In one story, a pirate captain killed one of his men and the sailor's ghost now guards the treasure. Then there is the story of the devil's watchdog, a huge dog with fiery red eyes that keeps watch over the island. For two hundred years, there have been reports of men in red coats and mysterious lights on the island. People

Oak Island today, as seen from the Oak Island resort.

have been afraid to investigate because, according to one legend, anyone who does is never seen again.

One of the most frustrating legends has led to the superstition that everyone must be absolutely silent while digging or the spell of the treasure will be broken. The story goes something like this: After hours of back-breaking work with no one breathing even a word, treasure hunters finally find a wooden chest! In the excitement of the moment, one of them yells out,

Curse of Oak Island

For more than two hundred years people have been searching for treasure on Oak Island. There have been accidents, unusual problems with equipment, and weird weather conditions. Many have risked their entire fortune to continue digging, and lost it all. But no matter the cost, people are ready to pay, even with their life, to solve this mystery.

To this day, no treasure has been found and some people say that there must be a curse on Oak Island. What else could explain all of the accidents and problems? No one knows the origin, but the curse says, "When all the oaks are gone and seven have died, the treasure will be found." Six people have already died, but the search continues.

An aerial view of Oak Island, showing Smith's Cove in the foreground, the path leading to Borehole 10X, and the Money Pit. Centre-left is the big swamp, centre-right is Fred Nolan's property and dock, and the causeway is in the background.

"That's it!" With those two words, the treasure vanishes.

Would you be brave enough to risk meeting the ghost of a dead pirate or the devil's watchdog? Who hid the treasure, and what did they hide? Check out the next chapter to learn some of the theories of what lies buried on Oak Island.

Chapter 1

Treasure Theories

"Every new attempt to solve the mystery has made it more puzzling." –R. V. HARRIS, THE OAK ISLAND MYSTERY

No one knows what is hidden on Oak Island or why someone went to so much trouble to hide it there. Some say that it would have taken, at the very least, a crew of over one hundred people an entire summer of hard work to dig the hole and create all of the tunnels, traps, and drains that continue to flood the Money Pit. What did they hide? Where exactly on the island is it? When and why was something hidden on Oak Island? The biggest question that people have been asking for two hundred years is, who did it? Here are some of the most common theories about where the Oak Island treasure may have come from.

Oak Island's First People

The Mi'kmaq, the Vikings, and the Acadians may have visited or lived on Oak Island. Did one of these groups bury treasure in the Money Pit?

(Left) A Mi'kmaw warrior. (Right) An Acadian family in the year 1640.

The region's aboriginal people, the Mi'kmaq, lived in this area, now known as Nova Scotia, thousands of years ago. They would spend their summers fishing along the coast and the winter inland, hunting and hunkering down. They travelled often and didn't own or carry anything they didn't need. Historians say that the Mi'kmaq would have no reason to go to such an effort to hide anything, but some think that since the Mi'kmaq spent their summers around Mahone Bay, they could have built the Money Pit.

A re-creation of a Viking settlement at L'Anse aux Meadows in Newfoundland.

The Vikings, skilled sailors from northern Europe, landed on the coasts of Newfoundland and Nova Scotia about one thousand years ago—five hundred years before other Europeans such as Christopher Columbus, John Cabot, and Samuel de Champlain came to North America. The Vikings spent the winters in L'Anse aux Meadows, Newfoundland, and there is evidence that they brought everything from cattle to spinning wheels with them when they crossed the Atlantic Ocean. Some say that the oak platforms found in the Money Pit are the remains of a Viking ship that plunged into a sinkhole. Could there be Viking treasure deep under Oak Island?

Did the Acadians hide something on Oak Island? In 1755, a tragedy occurred. Thousands of Acadians living in Nova Scotia were expelled, or forced to leave their land.

Even though they promised not to take sides in the war between England and France, their English rulers sent them away to places like France, the Caribbean, and southern parts of America. Years later, many Acadians walked all the way back from the southern United States to return to their former home. Some families walked back from the state of Louisiana, a three thousand-kilometre journey! Did they travel all that way to reclaim what they left for safekeeping in the Money Pit?

A tapestry, or woven rug, showing a Templar Knight.

Knights Templar and Freemasons

Knights Templar fought to keep the Holy Land— the area of the present-day countries of Israel, Jordan, Lebanon, the State of Palestine, and parts of Syria—from the Muslims during the Christian Crusades from the years 1100 to 1300. To join and become one of these elite soldiers, you had to surrender everything of value that you owned. Before long, the Templars had a bigger army and more money than some entire countries. Many people think that the Knights Templar were the guardians of the Holy Grail (the cup that Jesus used at the Last Supper), the Ark of the Covenant (the gold-covered chest thought to hold the Ten Commandments), and many other priceless religious treasures. To keep their treasure safe, some say the Knights loaded it on to ships and took it to Scotland.

There is evidence that Scottish noble Henry Sinclair sailed to Nova Scotia in 1398. Some think he hid the treasure of the Knights Templar there. Did he build the large castle that people claim once existed near Oak Island? It is said that his castle was at New Ross, up the Gold River, which empties into Mahone Bay only three kilometres from Oak Island. Some say that Henry Sinclair planted oak trees there as a guide to help his friends find their way.

Some think that the Knights Templar gradually

Knights Templar Bankers

Templar Knights created the first banks and invented cheques, or letters of credit. Giving pilgrims (travellers) a place to store their money protected them from bandits, who were out to steal from them.

changed into another secret society called the Masonic Order, during their time in Scotland. Members of the Order are known as Freemasons or Masons. The Masonic Order has been around in various forms since the early 1700s and is based on the craft of the stonemasons.

A Freemason coin showing Masonic symbols, including the all-seeing eye, a symbol of watchfulness, and tools for the stonemasons' work.

A stonemason was a highly skilled worker who shaped large pieces of rock into stones of the exact size and shape needed to make sturdy bridges, churches, and other buildings. Today, members of the secret society help the less fortunate and each other.

Many of the searchers and investors active on Oak Island in the 1800s and 1900s were Masons. Some people think that the rock formations and carvings found on stones on the island are symbols of the Masonic Order. Have the Masons been keeping a big secret? Is the treasure of the Knights Templar waiting to be found on Oak Island?

Spanish Treasure

Many searchers believe that Oak Island contains treasure that Spanish explorers plundered from the New World.

From the 1500s to 1700s, the Spanish explorers looted the coasts of Central and South America and the Caribbean islands. English explorer and privateer Sir Francis Drake sailed the coast of South America to raid Spanish ships filled with gold, silver, and jewels. When his ship, the *Golden Hind*, was filled with treasure he returned to England by sailing west. He first crossed the Pacific and then the Indian Ocean by sailing around the continent of Africa.

Sir Francis Drake, the second-richest pirate of all time. In England, he was a hero. In Spain, he was known as the pirate *El Draque*, or "the Dragon."

Pirate or Privateer?

What's the difference? Both raided ships, took captives, and kept whatever treasure they found on board. Privateers were working for their country and were supposed to give the plunder to their king. Pirates divided the loot among their crew and kept the biggest share for themselves.

Crossing the Atlantic

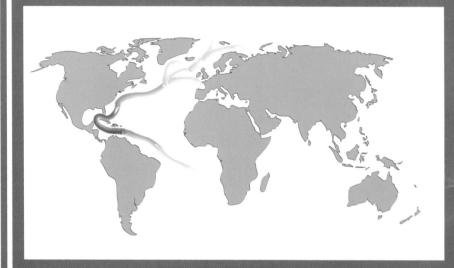

The quickest route for ships sailing from the Caribbean to Europe is to follow the Gulf Stream, an ocean current that helps them cross the Atlantic Ocean faster. Instead of heading straight across the Atlantic, ships use the Gulf Stream to sail north up the coast of North America and then east to Europe.

Crossing the Atlantic was very dangerous. Hundreds of Spanish ships never returned home. When this happened, people in Spain said that the ship disappeared *en el Golfo*, which is Spanish for "in the middle of the gulf" or ocean.

The water off of Nova Scotia's Sable Island is known as the Graveyard of the Atlantic, since it is so dangerous. Here the cold Labrador Current meets the warm Gulf Stream, creating rough waters and lots of fog. At least 250 ships have sunk off Sable Island, which is 350 kilometres from Oak Island. Is it possible that the captain of one of these lost Spanish ships tried to keep some treasure for himself by hiding it at Oak Island before sinking in the middle of the ocean?

Oak Island

This voyage took three years and made Sir Francis Drake the first European to sail around the globe.

For nearly ten more years, Drake continued to plunder the treasures of the New World, raiding almost any ship that he happened to find. Some think that he stopped off on Oak Island to hide some of his treasure and to repair his ships. The logs from his voyages don't mention stashing treasure at Oak Island…but would *you* include that information in the official record?

British Army and the Siege of Havana

In June of 1762 England attacked the Spanish port of Havana, in the country we now call Cuba. Even though

The Havana Harbour in 1762, where dozens of Spanish ships were captured.

the people of Havana were caught by surprise, they held off the invaders for two months. They may have even outlasted them if more English ships hadn't arrived. England attacked and conquered the entire city, taking all of the money and riches of the people and the church, and even from the Spanish ships in the harbour. The booty plundered from Havana was divided between the leaders of the English forces and some historians think that a few of those leaders may have kept a lot of the treasure for themselves.

One writer describes a secret plot where a ship bound for Havana actually sailed to Oak Island. The crew of highly skilled engineers and workers were told that their secret mission was to build a safe place to store

Havana Treasure, Found?

A man from the Mahone Bay area once told a local newspaper about the time, nearly one hundred years ago, when his grandmother showed him a wooden chest with twenty white canvas bags inside. His grandmother never let him peek inside the bags but he was sure they were filled with gold. He knew the bags were full of treasure because he remembered hearing that his grandfather had a sudden turn of good fortune, as if he might have found a treasure chest. Is it a coincidence that the man's grandfather was a relative of Anthony Vaughan, one of the people who first dug for treasure on Oak Island in 1795? Were these twenty white canvas bags the same ones looted from Havana in 1762?

ammunition for the soldiers based in nearby Halifax. They spent the next year sinking shafts and excavating tunnels. They protected their work with a complex system of booby traps that would prevent the enemy from ever getting at the ammunition. Meanwhile in Havana, ships were being loaded with spare ammunition and booty to be sent to England. The holds were filled with coconut fibre to cradle the cargo (see sidebar on page 36). Some chests were packed with cannonballs and others were filled with white canvas bags full of treasure.

As part of the plot, one of these English ships bound for home was redirected to Oak Island. When it arrived, the crew waiting there carefully moved the cargo into the prepared shafts and tunnels. They had no idea that the heavy chests that they buried held gold, silver, and jewels—not cannonballs and guns! The masterminds of this plot planned to keep the treasure hidden until they could return to dig it up. Did they die before they could return to Oak Island?

French Crown Jewels

One popular theory is that Oak Island holds the crown jewels of France or vast sums of money belonging to the King of France. Was the money that was meant to pay the soldiers at the French Fortress of Louisbourg hidden four hundred kilometres away, on Oak Island, to keep it safe from the enemy?

In 1791 King Louis XVI and his wife, Marie Antoinette, fled France with all that they could load on to a ship. When they were captured, they had no jewels. Is it possible that a lady-in-waiting was able to get the jewels to Louisbourg or maybe to Oak Island?

What's in a Name?

Some believe that the Money Pit contains priceless historic documents, not gold and jewels. The theory is that the original handwritten copies of William Shakespeare's plays are preserved in mercury and guarded by flood tunnels and booby traps deep under Oak Island. But why would anyone go to such trouble to hide manuscripts?

William Shakespeare was an actor who became famous for writing poems and plays, such as *Romeo and Juliet* and *Hamlet*, that people are still reading, studying, and watching five hundred years later. Shakespeare left school at age thirteen, so some people think that he could not have written these plays because they were complicated and often set in distant lands.

Oak Island

(Left) William Shakespeare. (Right) Sir Francis Bacon.

But Shakespeare could have loaned his name to someone else, something many people did back then.

Some experts claim to have found messages hidden in the plays that show Sir Francis Bacon was the real author of Shakespeare's plays. Bacon was a well-known scientist, lawyer, and politician. Did he write the plays and let Shakespeare take the credit? Bacon also hinted in some of his other writing that people would learn some amazing facts about him long after his death. Interestingly, Bacon owned land in Newfoundland and had friends with land in Nova Scotia. As a scientist and inventor, he could have engineered the flood tunnels

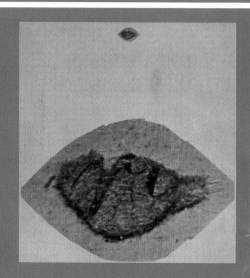

Mystery Parchment

On September 6, 1897, searchers at Oak Island gathered to review the findings of several holes that had been drilled down to fifty-three metres deep. When all of the mud and rock brought up by the drill was carefully checked, there were pieces of oak and iron and unusual looking pieces of stone. Tests proved that the stone was a type of man-made cement. But that wasn't the most exciting discovery. Using a magnifying glass they found something else, no bigger than a grain of rice. To everyone's astonishment, it was a piece of parchment with two letters written in dark ink. To this day, no one knows if the letters are "vi," "ui," or "wi." To the searchers it was proof that the Money Pit contained priceless historical documents.

that guard the Money Pit and made it tricky enough so that it would take hundreds of years for people to figure out the secret. Two things *are* certain: Bacon wrote about how to preserve parchment, a type of paper made from the skin of sheep, in mercury, and he loved puzzles. Is it a coincidence that a small piece of parchment was found in the Money Pit, or that an old dump on Oak Island had thousands of broken containers of mercury, or that in 1937 a digger found mercury on a drill that had just come up from the bottom of the Money Pit?

A view of Oak Island from the mainland, looking mysterious and tantalizing with the morning mist and a faint rainbow. What do you think is hidden there?

"That is more convincing evidence of buried treasure than a few gold doubloons would be. I am satisfied that either a treasure of immense value or priceless historical documents are in a chest at the bottom of the Pit."

—FREDERICK BLAIR, TORONTO TELEGRAM, APRIL 22, 1930

After two hundred years of searching, people are convinced that something of great value is hidden on Oak Island. Many hope that pirate treasure is still there, waiting to be found.

Chapter 2

Pirate Gold

"I've buried my money where none but Satan and myself can find it, and the one that lives the longest takes all."
—BLACKBEARD

Everyone knows that pirates captured ships full of gold and jewels, but what did they do with the treasure? It is also known that buried treasure has been found up and down the Atlantic coast. Did pirates hide their loot on Oak Island?

Captain Kidd (1645 or 1654–1701)

Captain William Kidd was born in Scotland and took to the sea at an early age. Little was known about him

Treasure Sites

Treasure has been found close to Oak Island and around Atlantic Canada. Nearly 150 years ago, a farmer in nearby Lunenburg found about two hundred French and Spanish coins from the 1700s under the floor of his barn. There are also stories of treasure being found on Isle Haute, in the Bay of Fundy, and in New Brunswick and Prince Edward Island. Some say that treasure has been found on Hobson's Nose, Graves Island, and Blue Rocks, all places close to Oak Island.

While no one has admitted to finding treasure on Oak Island, Anthony Graves, one of the island's long-time residents, is known to have paid for food and clothing with very old silver coins. Some people think that the treasure was found and shared by the original three treasure hunters and that their families have been keeping the secret since 1795.

Captain William Kidd, as imagined by Howard Pyle. The artist's pirate drawings from the late 1800s and early 1900s served as a model for pirate costumes in movies and books.

until his arrival in New York in 1689. For the next ten years he sailed both sides of the Atlantic, capturing enemy ships and turning the spoils over to the Crown. It isn't known if he got greedy or lost control of his crew, but in 1697 he began raiding coastal cities and pillaging ships—and not just enemy ships!

For the next two years Captain Kidd earned his reputation as a fearless pirate,

Treasure Maps

Some people claim to have a map showing where Captain Kidd buried his treasure. Many of these maps are very similar to the one found in the novel *Treasure Island*, written by Robert Louis Stevenson in 1883. Some people believe the book is based on Oak Island.

There are stories of Oak Island treasure maps being found in the false bottoms of old sea chests or hidden behind mirrors. Some Oak Island searchers have even travelled great distances to check out the claims. So far, no map has ever led to the Oak Island treasure.

sailing around the Indian Ocean and capturing huge amounts of treasure. It is well known that he buried some of his treasure to keep it safe. When he was in jail for **piracy** and murder, he offered to lead people to it. But William Kidd was hung on May 23, 1701, without telling anyone where he stashed his loot.

Did Captain Kidd come to Nova Scotia? Some say that there is no evidence of him sailing north of Boston. Others point out that his shipmates raided Port Royal, Nova Scotia, and Saint John, New Brunswick. In any case, Captain Kidd is the pirate most people associate with Oak Island.

Henry Morgan (1635–1688)

Henry Morgan was a successful pirate and privateer who became the governor of Jamaica. He was born near Cardiff, Wales, in Great Britain. He sailed out of Port Royal, Jamaica, at the time when pirates ruled the Caribbean, and is known for his bold raids. Morgan sometimes worked for the Crown but was known for ignoring the rules of war and raiding cities and ships when he thought that there was plunder to be had.

During one of his most famous raids, Morgan and his crew attacked Panama City, one of the richest and largest cities in the western world. Panama City was

Captain Henry Morgan was also known as "Barbadosed."

the place where all of the gold mined in the area was gathered and prepared for shipment to Spain. Some writers think that Morgan snuck away after the Panama raid and took most of the treasure with him. While no one knows how much loot Morgan got, the gold and silver could have been worth millions of dollars. Many treasure seekers think that Morgan buried the loot in the Money Pit.

Blackbeard (? –1718)

Edward Teach, the pirate known as Blackbeard, was born in Bristol, England, but no one is sure when. He sailed and plundered the coasts of North America and is remembered for his fearsome appearance: his face was almost hidden by his huge, bushy black beard, and it is said that he liked to hang pieces of burning rope from his hat to scare his victims. Blackbeard was a very successful pirate who captured many ships but had a reputation for setting most of the crew free.

In his last fight, Blackbeard proved nearly impossible to kill. British naval

A portrait of Blackbeard with flaming rope.

The Dying Pirate

Many people living in Nova Scotia in the late 1700s would have come from the Boston and New York areas and would have known that Captain Kidd liked to bury his treasure. At this time way before TV and the Internet, storytelling was a popular activity. A favourite Nova Scotia story about the dying pirate goes something like this: An old pirate lies on his deathbed with his nephew by his side. He has just finished telling his last remaining relative about sailing with Captain Kidd. Now that he is dying, he knows that he has run out of time to go back to get his share of the loot hidden many years ago. With his last breath, the old pirate tells his nephew exactly where to find the treasure.

BURIED TREASURE / LE TRÉSOR ENFOUI

To make the ending even more exciting, the person telling the story would claim that *he* is the old pirate's nephew. He then would end the story by saying that his biggest regret in life is that he never had the chance to go find the treasure, but that he can still describe exactly where it is and that it is close to where they are right now.

Stories similar to this one were told around Nova Scotia in the 1800s, keeping alive the idea that there was buried treasure nearby, just waiting to be found.

commander Lieutenant Robert Maynard vowed to stop the pirate. While hand-to-hand fighting on board his ship, the *Pearl*, Maynard managed to shoot Blackbeard, but the pirate kept fighting. Blackbeard later died trying to shoot the British sailors. At the end of this bloody battle,

Blackbeard's head was displayed on Maynard's ship as a warning to other pirates.

Although there is no evidence to show that Blackbeard sailed as far north as Nova Scotia, many people think he buried some of his pirate booty there.

Sir William Phips (1651–1695)

William Phips was a ship's carpenter, captain, and privateer. He is famous for discovering the wreck of the Spanish treasure ship *Concepción* in 1687. After recovering the millions of dollars' worth of silver coins, gold dust, pearls, and emeralds on board, he sailed to England with the loot and gave the biggest share of the silver to the king. As a reward, he was knighted. Sir Phips then returned to New England, where he acted more like a pirate by attacking and plundering nearby Acadia (today's Nova Scotia). He raided and looted the settlement at Port Royal on the Bay of Fundy. Then he attacked and burned the settlement of La Have, located forty kilometres from Oak Island.

Some writers think Sir William Phips stopped at Oak Island to hide some of the treasure from the *Concepción* before sailing to England. They say that he raided Acadia

Sir William Phips, who became the first governor of Massachusetts Bay.

so that he had time to go back to Oak Island to dig up the treasure. The value of the treasure from this ship could be worth $240 million today and only a very small portion of it was turned over to the Crown.

We know that there were pirates who sailed the Atlantic, close to Oak Island, and that pirates were known for hiding their loot. Did a pirate bury his or her booty in the Money Pit? No one knows, yet. But people have been searching for pirate treasure on Oak Island for more than two hundred years. Read the next chapter to find out more about the island's first treasure hunters.

Chapter 3

Searching For Treasure

"Vastly more money has been poured into [Oak Island] than anything of value ever secured from it."
–LIONEL AND PATRICIA FANTHORPE, THE OAK ISLAND MYSTERY

As we read in the introduction, the search for buried treasure on Oak Island began in 1795, when Daniel McGinnis found a tackle block in the branches of an oak tree. With help from his friends John Smith and Anthony Vaughan, and possibly Samuel Ball, he started digging in the shallow, round hole underneath the block and tackle.

At first, the digging was easy, a sure sign that someone had buried something. Close to the surface they found a layer of flat rocks. Three metres down was a carefully built platform of oak logs. After more digging they found a second oak platform and

Who was Samuel Ball?

Samuel Ball was a freed black slave from South Carolina who farmed on Oak Island until his death in 1845 at age eighty-one. In some descriptions of finding the Money Pit in 1795, Samuel Ball is included as one of the original diggers.

A painting of the Money Pit, as imagined by many treasure hunters.

then a third. The three platforms were about three metres apart and built right into the hard sides of the hole. Once they were nine metres from the surface, they knew that they could not dig any deeper by themselves. They needed help to find the treasure they thought must be there. Why would anyone dig such a deep hole if not to bury a something very valuable?

Daniel and his friends may have tried to get help, but people were either too busy, didn't believe the story of buried treasure, or were just plain scared. Everyone in the area heard the tales of mysterious lights and of curious people never returning from Oak Island. So if only the diggers knew about what they found, maybe they kept it a secret?

Both Daniel and John eventually settled on Oak Island and Anthony lived on the mainland not far away.

Today you can still see the stones that are part of the foundation of Daniel McGinnis's house on Oak Island.

Oak Island

For the next few years they farmed, but they never gave up their search. Small finds, such as a coin dated 1713, must have convinced them that there was treasure waiting to be found. There would be no more digging done on Oak Island for nearly ten years after they first made their discovery, but many others would follow in the boys' footsteps. Let's look at a history of the biggest treasure hunts on Oak Island.

History of the Big Searches

ONSLOW SYNDICATE (1804–1805)

Simeon Lynds heard the story of the treasure and formed the Onslow Syndicate in 1804 to raise money for

What Has Been Found on Oak Island?

- 2 ivory boatswain's, or bosun's, whistles
- 1 leather shoe
- 1 axe
- 1 pair of three hundred-year-old scissors
- several coins
- links from a gold chain
- 1 brass buckle
- broken pieces of china dishes
- 1 piece of parchment with the letters "vi," "wi," or "ui"

Charcoal, Putty, and Coconut Fibres

Tests showed that the putty had been man-made and that the grassy fibre was husks or fibre from the shell of coconuts. To this day, no one knows why the original builders put these things at regular intervals in the Money Pit.

Robert Restall used a pickle jar to collect samples of coconut fibre, now part of the collection of the Museum of Natural History in Halifax.

The closest coconut tree is more than two thousand kilometres from Nova Scotia. The fibre could have come from the holds of ships since it was commonly used as packing to keep cargo from shifting in rough seas. But who put it nearly two metres under the stones on the beach in layers twenty to sixty centimetres deep? It is thought that the coconut fibres are an important part of the system of drains that help to flood the Money Pit.

a search. The original diggers, McGinnis, Smith, and Vaughan, were a part of this group.

The Onslow Syndicate made the first of many unusual discoveries in the Money Pit in 1805. At the nine-metre level, they found a layer of charcoal on top of the oak logs. At the twelve-metre level, they found a layer of putty on top of the oak platform. At fifteen metres, they found a layer of smooth beach stones. At eighteen metres, there was a layer of grass-like fibre. At twenty-one metres, there was another layer of putty.

The Money Pit as it looked in 2010.

At twenty-seven metres, or ninety feet, from the surface, they discovered a large, flat stone covered with mysterious markings. It weighed about eighty kilograms and measured sixty centimetres long by thirty-eight centimetres wide and twenty-five centimetres thick.

The stone was grey and looked different from rocks found in the area. No one could read the symbols, so they didn't know what to do with it. John Smith ended up using it as part of his fireplace when he built his house on Oak Island. Many people saw the stone there but no one could figure out what it meant.

Searching for Treasure

The Inscribed, or Ninety-Foot, Stone

Around 1866 the Inscribed Stone, also called the Ninety-Foot Stone, was taken to Halifax where it was put on display in a store belonging to an Oak Island investor. A university professor deciphered it, but people have said that he was just part of a stunt to help raise money for the search. Some say that the words on the stone were instructions on how to block the flow of water into the pit. Others say that the stone provided directions to thirty-two different locations on Oak Island where treasure was buried.

Around 1919 the stone disappeared. It is too bad that no one ever took a photo, or that no exact description exists of the inscribed stone. Check out the photo above to see a **replica** of what people think the stone looked like. Most researchers think that the stone says, *Forty feet below two million pounds are buried.*

Beneath this stone the ground was muddy. When they probed the bottom of the pit, they found something hard. They left thinking that they would return in the morning to dig up treasure chests. But the next day, the shaft was full of water. They were the first group to discover the Money Pit booby trap. They tried to pump out the water but the pump burst. The next summer they dug a new shaft four metres away and tunnelled toward the Money Pit from thirty-three metres deep. As they got close to the pit, the shaft filled with water and the mud walls began to collapse. Lucky to escape alive, they admitted defeat and gave up the search.

TRURO SYNDICATE (1849–1850)

Early in the summer of 1849, the crew of the Truro Syndicate used an auger to drill a series of five holes in the Money Pit. The first two holes found nothing. The third hole struck the platform at thirty metres. Then the drill went through ten centimetres of oak followed by fifty-five centimetres of metal pieces. Surely this was a big treasure chest filled with gold coins! When the crew sifted through the mud, there were no coins, just three links from a chain. They dug deeper and what they found convinced them that there was a second treasure chest! They dug another hole and came close to what had to be the sides of the treasure chest. When they checked the auger, they found some brown fibrous stuff, much like a clump of dried grass.

It was James (or John) Pitblado's job to check through all of the mud and dirt that came up with the auger and to look for any traces of treasure or clues. When the auger brought up dirt from the fifth hole, Pitblado noticed something. Quickly, he picked it up, washed it off, and tucked it into his pocket. Someone noticed and asked what he found. Pitblado said that he would show everyone later and the crew returned to work. That night, Pitblado left Oak Island and never told the crew what he found. He did tell one person and the two of them tried to buy part of Oak Island. What did Pitblado find? No one knows, but it must have been good!

In 1850 the Truro Syndicate dug three more shafts that all filled with water. They built a cofferdam,

Booby Traps, Cofferdams, and Artificial Beaches

When the Truro Syndicate discovered drains on Smith's Cove in the 1850s, people were amazed. A series of five drains, shaped like a fan or the spread-out fingers of your hand, were buried deep under rocks, sand, eelgrass, and coconut fibres. These drains fed salt water from the ocean down into the Money Pit and are one of the most ingenious of all of the booby traps: when the diggers reached a certain level, water would flood into the pit, preventing any further work. To this day no one knows exactly how the water gets in or, more importantly, how to keep it out.

To create this drain system, the original builders of the Money Pit must have constructed a cofferdam. This would have kept the shore dry so that the drains could be built. Once the work was done, everything was covered, creating an artificial, or man-made, beach at Smith's Cove.

(Left) Smith's Cove in 1897. (Right) Smith's Cove today.

excavated the beach at Smith's Cove, and discovered that the original builder of the Money Pit had created a series of five drains under the beach. These drains, or flood tunnels, carried sea water deep into the pit, creating the perfect booby trap to keep the treasure safe.

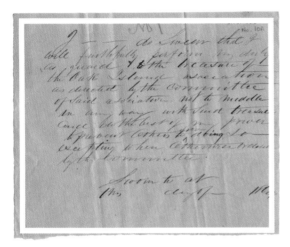

In 1864 a worker had to sign this oath and agree to "faithfully perform my duty as guard to the treasure of the Oak Island Association," and "not to meddle in any way with the said treasure and in the best of my power to prevent others from doing so...."

OAK ISLAND ASSOCIATION (1861–1865)

"As we opened it, the water hurled rocks about twice the size of a man's head, with many smaller, and drove the men back for protection." –SAMUEL FRASER, OAK ISLAND ASSOCIATION MEMBER

About ten years after the Truro Syndicate left, the Oak Island Association formed. They cleaned out and fixed the sides of the original Money Pit and then dug two more shafts. At the bottom of the second shaft they tunnelled into the pit, but it filled with water.

They used a crew of sixty-three men and thirty-three horses to try to drain the shafts, but their efforts caused the platforms in the pit to give way and fall to the bottom. Later searchers believed that the platforms fell into a large hole below the shaft—yet another booby trap created by the original builders! The crew dug three more shafts. To try to keep the water from flooding the

Oak Island excavations in 1897.

Money Pit, they dug a tunnel all around it, but nothing worked and water rushed in once again. Inspectors said that it was too dangerous and all work was stopped.

ELDORADO/HALIFAX COMPANY (1866–1867)

The Eldorado Company, also called the Halifax Company, was formed in 1866. It was named after the mythical South American city of El Dorado, which was rumoured to be filled with gold and treasure. Members of this group were convinced they could conquer the

Cave-in Pit

In 1878 Sophia Sellers was plowing a field near her home on Oak Island when her oxen plunged into a giant hole that suddenly opened up right in front of her. Was this a natural sinkhole, part of an air shaft, or another place to remove dirt from the tunnels that fed water into the pit? No one knows the answer, but the fact that the Cave-in Pit is located on a direct line between the booby traps of Smith's Cove and the Money Pit seems like a big coincidence!

(Left) Cave-in Pit around 1976. (Right) Cave-in Pit today.

pit by building a cofferdam to keep the water out of the flood tunnels. They built a dam measuring nearly 4 metres tall by 114 metres long, but it was knocked down by the powerful waves of Mahone Bay. They confirmed that sea water was getting into the Money Pit. The group then dug narrow holes and tunnels and built supports to hold up the walls of the Money Pit. They quit after less that a year, when a cave-in made it too dangerous to keep working.

OAK ISLAND TREASURE COMPANY (1893–1900)

Frederick L. Blair first heard about Oak Island as a boy in Amherst, Nova Scotia. He then devoted sixty years of his life to finding the treasure. In 1893 he formed the Oak Island Treasure Company. He encouraged many people to each pay a small amount

Unfortunately, the lucky horseshoe on this sign didn't help the Oak Island Treasure Company.

of money for a share in any treasure that was found. Selling shares was a common way to raise money for a search. In 1900 he bought out all of the other investors and took complete control of the search for treasure on Oak Island. He was convinced that using the latest technology and important information gathered from past searchers were the keys to success.

The Oak Island Treasure Company started its search at the Cave-in Pit, but gave up when it flooded. They found pieces of metal and were sure that they would soon locate the treasure chests rumoured to be there. This group found the small piece of parchment we talked about in Chapter One, one of the most interesting finds of all. They continued drilling and searching for several years but didn't make any other big discoveries.

In March 1897 a member of the Oak Island Treasure Company, Maynard Kaiser, became the second victim of the curse. He died when the rope carrying him up from the bottom of the pit slipped off a hoist and he fell to the bottom.

"Death might not stop the efforts of the treasure seekers, but a lack of money would." –Mark Reynolds, The Mystery of the Oak Island Treasure

In 1898 the Oak Island Treasure Company workers realized that muddy water from the Money Pit was showing up in the South Shore Cove, just over seventy metres south of the Money Pit. How was this possible? They poured red dye into the pit and found that the dye appeared in the ocean about ninety metres from the beach at Smith's Cove. This confirmed that that ocean water had been getting into the Money Pit from at least these two places on different sides of the island. The dye tests were repeated in 1941 by Edwin Hamilton and again showed that the dye poured into the pit came up from the ocean floor in three places off Smith's Cove, nearly one hundred metres from shore. When the Michigan Group repeated the dye tests in 2014, dye poured into a shaft did not appear in the ocean—another Oak Island mystery.

Searches done from 1795 to 1899 were usually funded by interested people who had lots of money. By the 1900s, searching became incredibly expensive. Only rich individuals (see the next chapter for some examples) had enough money to hire crews and buy or rent big machines and costly equipment. If you had money, you could help fund the search in return for a share of any treasure found.

Old Gold Salvage and Wrecking Company/ Camp Kidd (1909)

Captain Henry Bowdoin formed the Old Gold Salvage and Wrecking Company and claimed that his crew of six men could find the treasure in only two weeks. He set up Camp Kidd, named after the famous pirate, to begin his search in the fall of 1909. He soon realized that it wouldn't be so easy. His crew spent the summer digging and trying to drain water from the pit. Frustrated, they tried drilling more than twenty-five small holes before running out of money.

When Fred Blair refused to give Bowdoin more time, things got nasty and their fight went public. Bowdoin

This 1909 group of searchers includes Franklin Roosevelt (with the pipe, right) and Captain Henry Bowdoin (front row, left).

How Many Holes Have Been Dug?

There have been hundreds of shafts and holes drilled deep into the ground on Oak Island. In addition, at least eight large craters, or surface **excavations**, have forever changed the landscape of the island. Since no detailed records were kept of the early digging on Oak Island, searchers often find holes dug by earlier treasure hunters. Today, no one is exactly sure where the original Money Pit was dug in 1795.

and Blair each told the media two very different stories about the Money Pit. Bowdoin is best known for two reasons. The first is that one of the investors he brought to help find the treasure was Franklin Roosevelt, the man who would become the president of the United States in 1933. The second is what he said about Oak Island in a well-known American magazine called *Collier's* on August 19, 1911: "There is not and never was a treasure buried at Oak Island. The mystery is solved."

Chapter 4
Adventurers

"Treasure hunters who are dedicated are a very suspicious lot, and perhaps with just cause. Who knows what could be at stake; it could be nothing, but also it could represent a vast fortune." –Fred Nolan, Treasure hunter and Oak Island resident

Daniel McGinnis, John Smith, and Anthony Vaughan, the first to dig the Money Pit, kept looking for the treasure for the rest of their lives and passed their interest on to their families. Some people think that Edward Vaughan, Anthony's great-grandson, found treasure on Oak Island in the 1930s and passed it on to his own son. Up until his death, John Smith believed that there was treasure buried on his property. He sold his Oak Island lots to Anthony Graves in 1857. Did Anthony Graves find some of the treasure? No one knows for sure, but there are stories that he purchased his food and clothing with old Spanish coins. Sophia Sellers, the

Oak Island excavation in 1947 with a warning sign left by Edwin Hamilton, who searched for treasure here from 1938 to 1943.

daughter of Anthony Graves, and her children controlled who searched for treasure on parts of the island up until 1935.

Let's take a look at some of the adventurers who searched for the Oak Island treasure.

Gilbert Hedden searched for only four years but some of his discoveries are still considered key today. In 1936 he found a piece of a boulder covered in writing. Stories the locals told about other stones with unusual marks were enough to keep him looking. Eventually he found another stone with writing that was different from anything found to date. Other finds include stones with drilled holes and rocks laid out to form unusual shapes and triangles.

The treasure hunters who came after Hedden used what he discovered to help guide their searches. He also discovered old wooden beams under water at Smith's Cove, which many think the original builders of the Money Pit used well before 1795. Hedden was close to losing his fortune and was forced to quit in 1938, but he remained interested in Oak Island until his death in 1974.

Mel Chappell started working on Oak Island in 1897 when he was ten years old. He worked with his father, William, who searched for treasure on Oak Island from 1896 to 1899 and again in 1931. Mel bought part of the island in 1950 and was involved in the search until his death in 1980. He sold his land to David Tobias in 1977.

One of Chappell's most embarrassing moments must have been in 1950, when he paid $35,000 to have a

Treasure hunting on Oak Island in 1931.

"Mineral Wave Ray" machine search the island for gold. The machine was about the size of a small microwave with a lens at one end and with wires, rods, and batteries inside. To find a precious mineral like silver or gold, you first put a small sample of the metal inside the machine. The inventor then walked around Oak Island until the box made a sound. Of course the machine signalled that there was metal underground.

Chappell was convinced and anxious to begin digging. He tried to bring a large steam shovel, an excavator with a huge scoop, on to the island, but the barge, a low, flat boat, carrying the shovel sunk just off Oak Island.

But Chappell wasn't put off by yet another example of the curse, and he eventually got the steam shovel on the island. Chappell dug in several areas where the machine showed that there was gold. But—you guessed it—they didn't find any treasure. Chappell was a victim of a hoax. To make things even worse, Gilbert Hedden had been scammed into using the same gold finder twelve years earlier.

Restall Family

"The Restalls were not your ordinary family. They had big dreams and a love of adventure. But they didn't just dream, they actually did things that were quite out of the ordinary." –Lee Lamb, daughter of Robert and Mildred Restall, Oak Island Family: the Restall Hunt for Buried Treasure

Robert Restall was convinced that he and his family would be the ones to find the treasure. Before moving to Oak Island, Robert and his wife, Mildred, were motorcycle stunt riders. The family toured with circuses and carnivals before settling in Ontario. That all changed when Robert, Mildred, and their two sons moved into very basic lodgings on Oak Island in 1959.

Ricky Restall riding drums of fuel to the Money Pit. Photo provided courtesy of his sister, author Lee Lamb.

Their approach was completely different than those who searched before. Most of their work was done with a pick, a shovel, and a thirty-year-old pump. With only these tools, Robert and his son Bobby were able

Reader's Digest Article

In January of 1965 the *Reader's Digest* magazine published an article called "Oak Island's Mysterious Money Pit." This article sparked the imaginations of people all over the world and inspired many people to become treasure hunters. You too can read a reprint of this famous magazine article with the new title, "Treasure Hunt," in the December 2014 *Reader's Digest* or search the Internet for the original version.

to discover parts of the fan- or finger-shaped drains that fed ocean water into the Money Pit. The Restall family's work on Oak Island was featured in the January 1965 *Reader's Digest* article that inspired many future searchers to devote their lives to the treasure hunt.

Tragedy strikes

August 17, 1965, started out like most other days on Oak Island. It was very hot, and there was a group of tourists

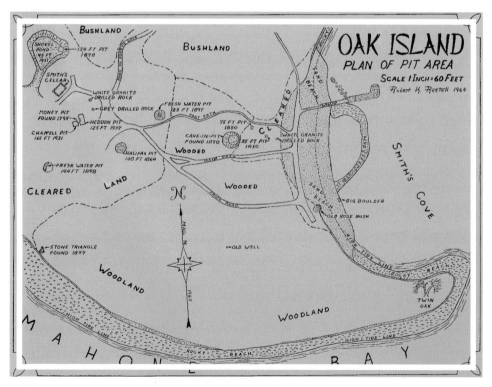

Robert K. (Bobby) Restall created and sold copies of this map of Oak Island for one dollar.

1704 stone

In the fall of 1960 the Restalls were uncovering some of the drains buried on the beach at Smith's Cove. Mildred and her nine-year-old son, Ricky, noticed something unusual on one of the stones. It looked like writing, and as the stone dried, the writing became clearer. Carved into the stone were four numbers: *1-7-0-4.* Could the people who buried treasure on Oak Island have carved it?

Some say the carving was made by earlier workers as a joke and was planted for someone to find. This could have been an example of "salting," which is when someone tries to trick others into finding something they have hidden. Some writers have said that some of the finds, like the 1704 stone, were planted to keep people searching for treasure on Oak Island.

close to where a small crew was clearing bush near the Money Pit. No one is sure exactly what happened first, but we do know that Robert Restall fell into or passed out at the bottom of a seven-metre hole. His twenty-three-year-old son, Bobby, went down and tried to rescue him. Then Karl Graeser, one of the workers, climbed down the ladder to help Robert and Bobby, but he passed out too. The other workers started shouting for help and then sixteen-year-old Cyril Hiltz tried to rescue the three men already in trouble. Andrew Demont was the

OAK ISLAND
MEMORIAL
1795 — 1995

IN MEMORY OF THOSE
WHO LOST THEIR LIVES
WHILE PURSUING THE
OAK ISLAND QUEST

UNKNOWN	1861
MAYNARD KAISER	MAR. 26, 1897
ROBERT RESTALL, Sr	AUG. 17, 1965
ROBERT RESTALL, Jr	AUG. 17, 1965
CYRIL HILTZ	AUG. 17, 1965
CARL GRAESER	AUG. 17, 1965

This tribute to the six dead treasure hunters is one of the first things tourists see on Oak Island.

next brave man down the ladder, followed by Leonard Kaiser. Finally some tourists arrived at the pit after hearing the commotion. Edward White, a fireman visiting from Buffalo, New York, knew that there had to be a problem with the air in the pit. He tied a rope to his waist, scrambled down the ladder and was able to rescue Leonard Kaiser and Andrew Demont.

Robert Restall, Robert Keith (Bobby) Restall, Karl Graeser, and Cryril Hiltz all died. Local man Jim Kaiser risked his life to go down into the shaft to bring up the bodies of four men that he had worked with. The official cause of death was drowning, but some say that it was the toxic carbon monoxide gas released from the old pump. Whatever the cause, this was the worst tragedy in the history of Oak Island.

Dan Blankenship was hooked on Oak Island when he read the *Reader's Digest* article in 1965. That summer he left his family and business in Florida and headed to Nova Scotia. For the next ten years he spent summers searching for treasure on Oak Island then headed south to work in Florida each winter. In 1975 he moved to Oak Island to live and search full time. Today, he is a consultant with the Lagina brothers on their reality show, *The Curse of Oak Island* (see pages 61–63). With over fifty years invested in Oak Island, some say Dan Blankenship is the most obsessive of all the searchers.

Robert Dunfield is the searcher who changed Oak Island more than anyone else. Starting in 1965, he used heavy equipment to dig craters of more than thirty metres across. He also tore up the beach at Smith's Cove and was responsible for the loss of some of the rocks that may have been important clues to finding the treasure. The biggest change was when he built a causeway from the mainland to the island in only ten days. The causeway was nearly two hundred metres long and was used to bring cranes and other heavy equipment to the island. Some have said that it was as if Dunfield

Borehole 10X

Borehole 10X is located fifty-five metres northeast of the Money Pit. Dan Blankenship spent years working this site thinking it might be a back door to the treasure. What started as a fifteen-centimetre-wide hole was expanded to over two metres across and over seventy-one metres deep with the sides reinforced by thick steel and concrete. Pieces of wood, metal, cement, charcoal, and broken chain have all been found in 10X.

Looking down Borehole 10x.

The most controversial thing about 10X is what cameras recorded there in 1971. Fuzzy black and white images showed what appeared to be treasure chests, a pickaxe, a severed human hand, and a dead body! None of this could be confirmed as the images were just not clear enough. Later searchers, including Dan himself, concluded that the video likely showed a worker's glove, not a human hand. A few years later, in 1976, Dan Blankenship almost died when the sides of 10X started to collapse with him near the bottom. Luckily, his son David was there to pull him up.

Tour guides will tell you that there are valuable things at the bottom of this hole—a few cameras and cellphones accidentally dropped by curious visitors who got a little too close to 10X!

was at war with Oak Island. After he finished digging, it looked liked an abandoned battlefield. Strange weather, accidents, and unexplained equipment problems caused many problems for Dunfield. Were these more examples of the Oak Island curse?

The two hundred-metre causeway, looking from Oak Island to the mainland.

Fredrick Nolan is a land surveyor who owns about one-quarter of Oak Island, or seven of the thirty-two lots. He became interested in the treasure in 1959 and has been actively searching ever since. He first tried to work with Mel Chappell and the main searchers, but when they turned him down he became one of their competitors. As a surveyor, Fredrick knew that in the past people used large rocks to mark the edges of property. He figured that the people who buried the treasure would also use boulders as guideposts. He started a careful search and found several cone-shaped boulders and stones with holes drilled into them. Next, he plotted the location of these stone markers on paper and drew lines between them.

Oak Island

Some of the lines formed an "X" or a cross, with the centre about 260 metres from the Money Pit. This formation has become known as Nolan's Cross.

When Nolan checked the ground at the centre point of the cross, he found the tip of a large boulder. Digging deeper, he was amazed to see that it was shaped like a human skull. There was another surprise: someone had carved the shape of a long knife or sword into the rock. The shape was an exact match for a knife that had belonged to Sophia Sellers, a long-time island resident.

Rick and Marty Lagina are brothers from the state of Michigan and the stars of The History Channel reality show *The Curse of Oak Island*. Marty, the younger brother, is a mechanical engineer and lawyer who got

Triton Alliance

"It has become more of an archeological and historical puzzle than a way to get rich." –David Tobias

David Tobias provided money to help the Restall search. By 1969 he formed a treasure-hunting group named Triton Alliance with himself as president and Dan Blankenship as field manager. They were named after Triton, a sea god from Greek mythology. The money behind this group came from people from all over Canada and the United States who gave funds to Triton Alliance with the hope of making even more money. Bill Sobey, of the grocery store chain, was one of the investors.

In 1970 they built a cofferdam that revealed evidence of an ancient wharf, called a **slip way**, that may have been made by the original builders of the Money Pit. The cofferdam couldn't stand up to the waves in Mahone Bay and eventually broke apart. The Triton Alliance spent millions of dollars digging, drilling, and using high-tech equipment on Oak Island.

In 1988 Triton Alliance planned to build a second cofferdam at South Shore Cove, but because it would cost millions of dollars and it might not withstand the tides and waves, they gave up on this idea. Who would have had the knowledge and enough skilled workers to create the drains and cofferdam at Smith's Cove more than two hundred years ago? And how did they do it? People are still trying to figure this out.

rich working in the energy business. Rick has been obsessed with Oak Island since reading about it in *Reader's Digest.* He is now retired and is devoting his time to finding the treasure. The brothers, along with their business partners, bought the part of Oak Island owned by David Tobias. Together the new owners are called the Michigan Group, and they control the treasure-hunting company Oak Island Tours Inc.

The first season of *The Curse of Oak Island* aired in January 2014. Dan Blankenship said that the *maravedi,* or old Spanish coin, that the Lagina brothers found was the first real evidence that there was someone on Oak Island before McGinnis, Smith, Vaughan, and Ball began to dig in 1795.

<hr />

Many adventurers have lost their entire fortunes searching for treasure on Oak Island. Some have spent fifty years or more digging and have only some odd stones or a few old coins to show for a lifetime of work. Even so, the lure of buried treasure and the hope of finding an immense fortune have kept people hunting for more than two hundred years. But all of this digging has taken a toll of the island. Many people feel that it is time to stop all work so that Oak Island's natural beauty will be preserved for future generations.

Conclusion
Plunder or Protect?

"I saw enough to convince me that there was treasure buried there and enough to convince me that they will never get it."–Isaac Blair, a workman at Oak Island between 1863 and 1867

After more than two hundred years of searching for treasure on Oak Island, there are more questions than answers. Who do you think did it? Why would someone hide treasure and not come back for it? Did they already remove it? Is the Money Pit just a decoy to keep people busy searching in the wrong place? Why can't modern technology find something that was hidden using very low-tech or primitive tools? How would you try to find it? Many people were certain that they had the solution to finding the treasure, but so far no one has been able to figure out the mystery.

How Did They Do It?

No one knows how the Money Pit was constructed or who did it. If people knew who dug the original hole, then there might be clues about how to get to the bottom and find the treasure. If it could be proven that it was dug by the British military or the Knights Templar or that the Freemasons are still guarding the treasure, then the

Finding Your Own Treasure

If Oak Island was a good place to hide treasure, might there be treasure hidden somewhere close to where you live? You can learn more about treasure hunting by checking out books available at your library. Or you can try searching the Internet with terms such as "buried treasure" and the name of your province or city. You will likely find many stories about treasure found in your area and tips on where to start your own search.

There really is treasure everywhere if you know where to look. Peek in the attic of you great-grandmother's house to see what your family may have stored away. That box of toys or old comic book might be worth a fortune now, and the stamps on those old letters could be valuable. Next time you are at the beach, check above the high-water mark. Move some sand and look: a piece of beach glass, a beautiful stone, or an old coin might be sitting right there. Check your own yard: if you find a shallow circular hole like Daniel McGinnis did, get a friend or two and start digging!

Conclusion: Plunder or Protect?

secret of Oak Island would probably have been revealed by now. There is no sure way to guess who did it or what they were hiding. We are left to wonder.

The Future of Oak Island

Curious people have been visiting Oak Island for more than two hundred years. Before the causeway was built in 1965, people would hire boats for the short trip to the island and have a picnic on the beach or near the digging sites. Tourists still flock to the island to see it for themselves. Now you can kayak in Smith's Cove and catch a glimpse of the big swamp. You can take a tour of the island and see the Money Pit and Borehole 10X. There are replicas of the Inscribed Stone and some of the things found on Oak Island at the Train Station in

The Michigan Group at work on Borehole 10X in the summer of 2015.

Oak Island

Chester, Nova Scotia, at the Oak Island resort, and at the museum on Oak Island.

Because of the careless way that some of the early work was done, the Inscribed Stone and some of the rock formations that may have been key to solving the mystery were lost. Many feel strongly that Oak Island should be kept as natural as possible and that all digging should stop. Some people think that an archaeologist should oversee all of the digging on the island to help preserve artifacts and clues to what may be buried on the island.

At the museum on Oak Island, you can see some of the tools that Dan and David Blankenship used to dig Borehole 10X. The display also shows a collapsed piece of the steel that once lined 10X (see page 59).

Conclusion: Plunder or Protect?

Area people have been earning a living from Oak Island since the 1800s. Some have been hired as diggers and others have loaned equipment or sold supplies to the searchers. People have rented out spare bedrooms or even their entire home to people who have come to search for treasure. There are stories that some of the things found during the digging were actually put there by local workers. This "salting" may have been done to keep the people in charge of the searches interested. Maybe finding a few links from a gold chain would keep the investors searching? And if the digging continued, then the workers would have jobs and paycheques. Others say that there is no way that any of the workers would have links from a gold chain that they would be willing to throw away.

Some people worry that if the treasure is ever found, the world will lose interest in the Money Pit. If that happens, there would be no reason for anyone to visit Oak Island, which would put many people out of work. But for now, the lure of the treasure is as strong as ever and the search is still on.

Oak Island Timeline

Pre-1795 someone may have hidden something on Oak Island.

1795 Money Pit discovered and dug by McGinnis, Smith, Vaughan, and Ball.

1804–1805 Onslow Syndicate finds charcoal, putty, coconut fibres, Inscribed Stone, and sets off the first booby traps that flood the pit.

1850 Truro Syndicate builds cofferdam and discovers the drains at the beach.

1861–1865 Oak Island Association's digging and tunneling causes a collapse, and work stops.

1861 Pump explodes killing one, the first victim of the curse.

1866 The Eldorado (Halifax) Company builds a cofferdam and proves that sea water is getting into the pit.

1878 Sophia Sellers falls into the Cave-In Pit when plowing a field near the Money Pit.

1893–1900 Oak Island Treasure Company uses red dye to prove that sea water flows into the pit.

1897 Tiny piece of parchment with two letters written in black ink is found in the pit.

1897 Maynard Kaiser is killed in a fall when a rope slips off a hoist.

1909 Captain Bowdoin forms The Old Gold Salvage Company, claiming he can find treasure in two weeks.

1931 William Chappell, Nova Scotia Committee, part of the Oak Island Treasure Company, digs deepest shaft yet (41 metres) but are slowed by many accidents.

1935–1937 Gilbert Hedden finds unusual stones that later searchers feel are important clues.

1938–1943 Edwin H. Hamilton, an engineering professor, drills for six summers and proves that the Chappell shaft is 1.5 meters from the original pit.

1959–1965 Restall Family lives and works on Oak Island.

August 1965 Four men are killed, bringing the Oak Island death toll to six.

October 1965 Robert Dunfield builds causeway, linking Oak Island to the mainland.

This sign, posted by Fred Nolan, is a warning to stay off his section of Oak Island. When tour guides point it out, they say that it should be taken very seriously. Rival treasure hunters, the Michigan Group and Fred Nolan, are not on friendly terms.

A booklet celebrating two hundred years of treasure hunting on Oak Island.

1966–1969 David Tobias pays for the cost of exploration and drilling work done by Dan Blankenship.

1969 Triton Alliance forms and over next 35+ years makes many small finds.

1976 Dan Blankenship, nearly killed in Borehole 10X, is saved by his son David.

1970 Triton Alliance builds a 122-metre cofferdam, revealing parts of an ancient wharf or slip way.

1995 Groundwater survey by Woods Hole Oceanographic Institution.

1996 Geological Survey of Canada explores possible sinkholes and shipwreck off Oak Island.

2006 Michigan Group buys part of Oak Island from David Tobias and forms Oak Island Tours Inc.

2008 Michigan Group begins work on Oak Island.

2012 Oak Island Tours Inc. is granted a five-year license to search for treasure on Oak Island.

2014 *The Curse of Oak Island* TV show begins on The History Channel.

Acknowledgments

Thanks to my husband, Nick Barry, for his enduring support while I devoted all of my attention to this project. My entire family, especially my children, Alex and Hope, patiently listened to lots of stories of buried treasure and helped me in many different ways. My sister, Pat Hamilton-Warr, even visited Oak Island with me and took some great photos. Dad, I wish you were here to see this!

I couldn't have completed this book without help from:
Nicholas, Alex, and Hope Barry
Ken Boehner
Emily Daigle
Dave Eisnor
Robert Frame
Patricia Hamilton-Warr
Jackie and Barry Hamilton
Danny Hennigar
Beulah Kaiser
Lee Lamb
Mahone Islands Conservation Association, especially
    Michael Ernst and John Meisner

Ben Peters

Staff of Nova Scotia Archives, especially Philip L. Hartling

Staff of Library and Archives Canada

Staff of the Museum of Natural History, especially Laura
Bennett, Lisa Bower, and Marion C. Munro

Staff of Nimbus Publishing, especially Jenn Embree, Whitney
Moran, and Patrick Murphy.

Staff of the Saint John Free Public Library and the Halifax
Public Library

And all of the authors, bloggers, experts, and curious people
who shared their ideas about Oak Island.

Glossary

auger: a type of drill whose blade brings material up and out of a hole.

block and tackle: rope-and-pulley device used to lift heavy loads.

boatswain's, or **bosun's**, **whistle**: a whistle used by an officer on a ship.

booby trap: a device used to stop an intruder.

borehole: a narrow shaft.

cofferdam: a temporary U-shaped structure built in a body of water. The water is then pumped out of one side to create a dry work area, where a permanent structure can be built.

Crown: the government of the time.

engineer: a person with specialized scientific training who solves problems or designs and builds engines, machines, computer systems, or structures such as roads or bridges.

excavation: a hole made by digging or scooping out earth.

extraterrestrial: a creature or object that is not from the planet Earth.

Oak Island

investor: someone who contributes money to a project with the hope of sharing in the profits.

lady-in-waiting: a woman who helps or assists a queen or princess.

manuscript: an author's work, before it is published or made into a book.

mercury: a heavy, silvery-white-coloured metal that becomes a liquid at standard temperature and pressure.

New World: the term used beginning in the 1500s by explorers, such as Christopher Columbus, referring to North and South America.

piracy: robbery on the sea.

plunder: to rob or steal. Can also refer to the "booty," or stolen goods.

raid: a surprise attack.

replica: an exact copy or reproduction.

shaft: a vertical tunnel dug from the surface down into the earth.

sinkhole: a hole in the surface of the earth caused when underground water erodes or removes rock and soil. The size of a sinkhole can range from one meter to over half a kilometer wide—and just as deep.

slip way: a sloping ramp used to launch a boat.

Recommended Reading

"There is more treasure in books than in all the pirates' loot on Treasure Island and best of all, you can enjoy these riches every day of your life." –WALT DISNEY

Information

Conlin, Dan. *Pirates of the Atlantic: Robbery, Murder and Mayhem off the Canadian East Coast.* Halifax: Formac, 2009.

Crooker, William S. *Oak Island Gold.* Halifax: Nimbus, 2001.

Crooker, William S. *Pirates of the North Atlantic.* Halifax: Nimbus, 2004.

Crooker, William S. *Tracking Treasure: In Search of East Coast Bounty.*Halifax: Nimbus, 1998.

Fanthorpe, Lionel and Patricia Fanthorpe. *The Oak Island Mystery: The Secret of the World's Greatest Treasure Hunt.* Toronto: Hounslow Press, 1995.

Finnan, Mark. *Oak Island Secrets.* Halifax: Formac, 1995.

Harris, Graham and Les MacPhie. *Oak Island and its Lost Treasure.* Halifax: Formac, 2013.

Harris, Reginald. V. *The Oak Island Mystery.* Toronto: McGraw-Hill Ryerson, 1967.

Lamb, Lee. *Oak Island Family: The Restall Hunt for Buried Treasure.* Toronto: Dundurn, 2012.

O'Connor, D'Arcy. *The Secret Treasure of Oak Island: The Amazing True Story of a Centuries-Old Treasure Hunt.* Guilford, Connecticut: Lyons Press, 2004.

O'Connor, D'Arcy. *The Big Dig: The $10,000,000 Search for Oak Island's Legendary Treasure.* New York: Ballantine, 1988.

O'Connor, D'Arcy. *The Money Pit: The Story of Oak Island and the World's Greatest Treasure Hunt.* New York: Coward, McCann, Geoghegan, 1978.

Reynolds, Mark. *The Mystery of the Oak Island Treasure: Two Hundred Years of Hope and Despair.* Toronto: Lorimer, 2011.

Sora, Steven. *The Lost Treasure of the Knights Templar: Solving the Oak Island Mystery.* Rochester, Vermont: Destiny Books, 1999.

Novels

Clark, Joan. *The Hand of Robin Squires.* Toronto: Clarke, Irwin, 1977.

Dinsdale, Christopher. *Betrayed: The Legend of Oak Island.* Toronto: Napoleon, 2009.

D'Entremont, Cynthia. *Oak Island Revenge: a Jonah Morgan Mystery.* Halifax: Nimbus, 2012.

Pritchard, J. J. *The Secret Treasures of Oak Island*. Halifax: Formac, 2002.

Walters, Eric. *The Money Pit Mystery*. Toronto: HarperCollins, 1999.

Want to learn more? Check out these websites:

chesterbound/Oak_Island.com

friendsofoakisland.com

oakislandmoneypit.com

worldtimeline.info/oakisland

oakislandtreasure.co.uk

Image Sources

Bridgeman Images: 17, 25, 28

Canada Post: 29

Canstock: 11, 15, 16, 21, 24, 27

Courtesy Dan Soucoup: 5

Erin Banks: 33

Franklin D. Roosevelt Presidential Library: 47

Joann Hamilton-Barry: 36 (with permission from the Nova Scotia Museum), 44, 71

Ken Boehner: 7, 8, 23, 34, 37, 38 (top), 40 (right), 57, 60, 66, 67

Courtesy Lee Lamb, from *Oak Island Family: the Restall Hunt for Buried Treasure*: 55

Library Archives Canada: 42, 52, 56

Natural Resources Canada: 3

Nova Scotia Archives: 22, 35, 40 (left), 41, 50

Parks Canada: 10

Courtesy Patricia Hamilton-Warr: 70, 43 (right)

Courtesy Richard Arthur Restall and Lee Restall Lamb: 54

Robert Frame: 59

Shutterstock: vi, 12, 14, 64

William S. Crooker: 2, 38 (bottom), 43 (left)

Index

Oak Island